MY TRUE BODY

MARK SOLOMON

MY TRUE BODY

MARK SOLOMON

HAVEL HAVULIM
NEW YORK CITY
Havel.Havulim@gmail.com

Cover artwork by Marylyn Dintenfass: CAME UPON A BURNING BUSH,
2012, Oil on canvas, 60 x 60 inches, Courtesy Driscoll Babcock, New York
Design by Sohrab Habibion & Alexandra Tagami
Mark Solomon photo: ©2016 Peggy Elliot
Marylyn Dintenfass photo: ©2015 Alvia Urdaneta
Cover artwork photo: ©2012 Tim Pyle

A NOTE ON THE TYPE:

The main text of this book is set in the Adobe Garamond font family, which is based
on the typefaces first created by the French printer Claude Garamond in the sixteenth
century. This serif face was created by Robert Slimbach and released by Adobe in 1989;
its italics are influenced by the designs of Garamond's assistant, Robert Granjon.

The titles and section heads are set in Optima, a typeface designed by Hermann
Zapf (1918-2015). Optima was inspired by classical Roman inscriptions
and is distinguished by its flared terminals: the ends of letters.

Published by Havel Havulim, New York City
Havel.Havulim@gmail.com
©2016 Mark Solomon
ISBN: 978-1-4951-9463-4
LCCN: 2016903215
First Edition

Printed in China by Regent Publishing Services Ltd.

TO THE MEMORY OF

Bob Simon
best friend since high school
1941-2015

and

Steve Kogan
best friend since college
1938-2015

"For we were nursed upon the self-same hill"

André Breton says in the *Second Surrealist Manifesto:*
"Everything tends to make us believe that there
exists a certain point of the mind at which life and
death, the real and the imagined, past and future,
the communicable and the incommunicable, high
and low, cease to be perceived as contradictions."

Quoted by Charles Simic
in *Dime-Store Alchemy: The Art of Joseph Cornell*

THE DISMAL PLAIN

ALL THE BLOOD I'LL EVER HAVE

THAT OTHER COUNTRY

JUST AS I AM

THE DISMAL PLAIN

THESE ARE THE STREETS

These are the streets where I used to walk my rage once I woke
            from the kick I gave the scrap-paper bucket underneath
                 the Big Boss Desk I had to sit behind in those days. Leaping
down the back stairs two, three at a time, rage pulled me, eight stories,
            just to yank me back and forth between the hydrant and the lamppost.
                 Over there was old Police Headquarters, pistol shops out back
selling handcuffs, ammo, weighted billy clubs. Across the street, first
            Krasilovsky's Safes, next Karl Otto's Tool and Die, and finally Zeke
                 the Machinist, wheels within wheels in the window spinning dizzy
combinations driven by thick belts, toothed gears, all off the single, central, endless
            worm-screw. And there's the window on Grand and Elizabeth where I'd always find
                 myself, no jacket in the winter drizzle, staring at the T-shirts—one
of Mussolini, another of Sophia—staring at the long-spouted bright tin olive oil cans,
            at the hand-painted cheap espresso cups, staring into the gloomy eyes of San
                 Gennaro, the blood in its phial gone liquid again, blaspheming black
Vesuvius bubbling over behind him. At the bar of The Villa Pensa I would lean
            on my elbows, sipping bitter coffee. I would study the twig of sugar crystals
                 growing in the golden Fior d'Alpi. I would bite into one of those twisted
black cigars you had to cut in half, smoke circling my eyes and nostrils, shrouding
            my anger just enough, Montovani from the hi-fi washing up like warm surf
                 over soft breasts of white beaches somewhere in my mind. Jo-Jo Favale
knew how to take good care of me. The pot of coffee finished, cigar chewed through,
            his sweetest waiter, Pepe from Trieste, would show me to the corner table—
                 flowers, cold glass of water, fresh bread in a basket, cold pats
of butter in a dish of ice, a steaming soup, thick with white beans and pastina.
            "Just like Mama make at home," he always said. "Come, take your place, Signore.
                 I'll go bring some wine." I would smooth the heavy linen napkin
open on my lap and bring my chair in close against the table.

NEW YEAR'S DAY

There is gentle Jacobean music.
Everyone looks familiar, friendly.
No one is sure of anyone's name, but
we're all good friends of the Charleses.

I furnish my refuge in the den—
cushioned easy chair, brandy, a book
of Adirondack photographs.
From crags of shale I admire
the cumulus rising
over soft forest ridgelines.
I gaze across lakes slashed with light.
Under tumbled boulders
I rummage crumbled wood.
My hearing has become exquisite.

A teenage girl opens
a book before the fire.
Through the furrow of shoulders,
soft hair pours down her back,
would flow over buttocks
into shallows between them
along smooth legs to creases
in jeans beneath her knees.

The fire suddenly slumps in,
crushing clusters of embers.
The child jumps away. I

flee my book, my drink,
look for my wife.

ARIZONA

Could I cry, "Oh my God!" in Arizona? Would
       that train grinding into town, containers
            of Pacific mildew—Hanjin, Sealand,
Evergreen—bolted down on flatcars in Seattle, make
       my bed jangle in the middle of the night? Maybe
            there's a gay bar or coffee shop in Bisbee
where desire is believed in, or a festival of fiber arts—
       strips of desert twisted into baskets, scratchy
            as whiskers, or soft mats I could wrap
myself in, fresh from the bath, against my dread
       of desiccation after forty. I know that place
            in Benson where boxcars rattle over
Highway 86, glass and rusted metal pressed
       to the divide. Once along that crumbled
            loading dock a woman in leather jacket
let down her hair in a yellow Chevrolet to hang
       upon a strange man's face. In my room,
            cold dry air sifted cinder-block dust
on my dinner in a foil tray, light shining in all night long.

I COME DOWN
AT MY BIRTHDAY PARTY
WITH A SUDDEN CHILL

The carved marble post the urinal provides
for me to lean on as I ease myself
is curved, inviting my caresses
like a naked woman's shoulder, though
its coldness drains warmth and strength
from my palm as if the stone
were thirsty for vitality.

          Blood is
slipping away from my face. A metal
taste sets up inside my throat. I'm
hearing the pummeling of a waterfall
within the chromium plumbing. I have
been soiling my trousers.

          Unzippered,
I stumble to a cubicle, shivering.
It cannot be the wine. I will sit a little while.
Perhaps my wife will send a friend to find me.

SWEETEST BABY
ON THE
HIGHEST MOUNTAINTOP

Baby on the mountain
heels sewn together
no messenger or god
smuggles you away.

Finally your human
smell and howl subside.
Animals eat you
then birds and flies.

This the beginning
not the end of your life
in the cradle
of your father's mind.

DOOR OF THE PATRIARCHS
for Aviva Green

Inside the Study House
thick volumes bound in hide
lie tumbled on tables:
olive, gray, the color
of dried blood, like the stones
outside along the wall,
the path that leads away
between high rows of cypress
from the low round yellow
Door of The Patriarchs.

Beyond the wall, sweet water
in The Women's Garden spills
through split bamboo, gathers
in a shallow pool rimmed with dark
tumescent leaves.
                              Hovering
orange birds plunge to gorge
nectar from the meaty flowers.

Under the leaves, eyeless
chrysalides silently pulse
fluids into folded wings.

TEDIOUS LANDSCAPE

Train compartment: child in my lap
on the verge of waking. I lean
near falling over into sleep.

We're traveling somewhere. I can't
understand the language, worn out
with strangeness. Yet I'm deeply

at home. My own mind, a tedious
landscape: void of any feature,
story, with meaning to me.

The people, their music, the food—
everything gray. Fish, syllables,
heavy dumplings. Rain, winter fields,

the broad swollen river. Child still
undifferentiated not
waking, no voice—face—in my lap.

A WOMAN WITH HIM

My father. Showing up. Again.
My dinner table, our '50s
backyard with my swings and sandbox,
here, a concert, across the aisle.

A woman with him, half his age.
Half MY age! She's caught me glaring,
passes a note: "Not your business!
He's dead! Does not know you exist!"

NEBRASKA

My kitchen light spreads along the wall.
        The sound I imagine: *Balk* . . . or . . . *Milk*.
                Like that. Slow. Click at the end.

Refrigerator door. The countertop pale,
        buttery yellow. Telephone on the wall
                nauseating, pointless, making me

crazy like mosquito bites along my knuckles
        nights when the sheets stick and I can't
                find sleep. She's passing through

"The Beef State" now. "We are on the way!"
        A picture postcard. Cattle. High dry plains.
                Windmill. Barbed wire for miles.

LEAVING HOME

First time. Seventeen. I leave my parents' home
      two nights before the high school graduation, pick up Judy, take her
          to Allenwood Park under the cedars where knotted roots
twist through the turf. My shoes still on, my pants still tangled about my ankles,
      I was finished before I even started but she pulled me down on top of her anyway
          and pushed my lips against her breast bared by her lifted sweater
and kissed my hair, whispering Woody Guthrie tunes, gazing up into the branches.

Second time. Thirty-four. I leave my first wife's home
      two weeks after our son's third birthday. I had the backyard finished,
          all the builders' rubble removed, a redwood deck built, the soil
conditioned with peat moss, manure, and vermiculite, a brick path laid
      through the rotten stink before the roses could be planted and the weeds
          begin to rise. I was working the family business. I published my first
few poems. I heard about my wife's affair. I slept with the woman who told me.

Third time. Fifty-one. My own home now.
      Words are inscribed on my doorposts and on my gates, bound for a sign
          upon my arm, for frontlets between my eyes. Words that I speak
when I'm sitting in my home, when I travel on a journey to The Land of the Patriarchs
      where that son, now twenty, diligently studies them. Fringes dangle
          from the corners of my garment, that I may look upon them and remember
not to follow the desires of my heart and of my eyes, which lead me
      astray. But the blood-rush presses at the threshold, floods words, letter after letter,
          rising to obliterate The Name.

A COMMENT ON MY HOST

What a relief to be speaking again, restored
        to life if only for a moment. This body I inhabit—reluctant,
                jealous—imposes strict, unpleasant regulations.

I don't blame him. I am careless, an ungrateful guest. I leave
        beds piled with their soiled linen, dishes
                in the sink, uncovered plates in the refrigerator.
I never remember to water his plants or to feed
        his ridiculous animals. I inhabit his body
                as if it were one of my own and I had many to spare.

I refused to go to Jerusalem with him. Oh, the weariness
        of sharing quarters with his holy son, wandering
                narrow ancient alleys in search of scribes and prophets,
handing out cold cash without distinction to tzaddikim
        and charlatans. I can sense the "pleasures" of his quests,
                his pleas and bargainings within and without.
Flakes of unleavened cakes still lodge in his folds,
        his ears still ring with mingled wails and hallelujahs,
                his blood charged with resolutions he should make,
the vows, the purpose of his circumcision and his precious seed.

        Tiresome. His wife can't stand him in this mode. The congregation
            where he worships in New York finds him
insufferable, uncommunicative, withdrawn beneath the large black-banded
        tallis he acquired in B'nai B'rak. He wanders his rooms,
                the streets and sidewalks, banished from his true home
amid the temporary shelters of the dismal plain, searching for someone
        who has seen what he has seen, known what he has known.

INCANTATION

If I can put on horns
        to make the Reindeer come

If I can shimmy at the edges of rivers
        to make the Salmon come

If I can cover my arms with feathers
        and stamp the earth to make the Eagle come

Why do You still leave me crying alone
        when I dance at Your mirror
            in Your jewels and Your dresses?

ALL THE BLOOD I'LL EVER HAVE

I WOULD MAKE LOVE WITH TREES

had I my true body, would
yield to their elaborate
caresses soothing open
my limbs and boughs, rending
gently my rough bark to receive
and be entered.

CHAVELE

Chava (Hebrew): "life-source." Eve in English.

Night holds
a bowl of milk
open under the moon.

My own
stiff bones
glide away.

Chavele,
Little Chava,
sister, ghost
sprung from my side,

return,
reopen me.

Re-member me.

CITY CHILDHOOD, 1943

Sudden flashing cloud!

Pigeon flocks curling into,
out of angled morning light.
Familiar roofs of Queens.

- - - - - - -

Knots of smoke.

Black smear. Poland's
stack and spire penetrated sky—
incandescent rags of bodies.

I REMEMBER

I remember
the night my father arrived.
The lights were out.
The willow fell.
We waited in the dark
for the all clear.
Mother demanded,
"Don't be afraid."

PYRO-BOY WITH WOODEN PLANE

Splintered ribs rip its dope-slick paper skin.
        Sweet glue squeezed from green and yellow tubes
                knits the broken body, the twisted wings.

Matchstick! I kiss the white bead at your bright red tip.
        Strike anywhere.
                Unlock my brilliant chaos.

DETECTIVE

The detective called Arthur, whose real name is Mordechai, suspects
     me of murder yet he pretends he suspects someone else. He asks me
         about a movie where a young man is hounded by an older one
along a high mountain road. The young man's car runs out of gas. He stuffs
     a few things in the pockets of his coat, gets out to walk as the older man
         pulls into view around a bend, looks over his shoulder, tries
to find a way down the steep side of the mountain.
     The scenery is vast and stunning: glistening peaks, white breasts, blue ice.
         There aren't any weapons, the young man is lucid, well built,
resourceful, intelligent, could easily answer any physical threat. He flees
     the older man for reasons I can only guess at. And Mordechai/Arthur over here
         grills me mercilessly, as if my very thoughts could help him understand.

What has the young man done, do you think? Why does he flee? Why didn't he go to
     the police? Isn't he going to get injured or killed walking around unprepared?
         Why do you suppose the old man is after him? Doesn't he simply want
to talk? Do you think the movie was made in Mexico? Did you know I was
     raised in Granada and spent my adolescence in the mountains? Do you think
         I look old? Do you think Alcibiades was cruel or unfair? Did your mother

ever put your penis in her mouth? Not once? Are you certain? Didn't you

murder a young man once? Or break his heart? Or was it a long time ago when you

were a student, and it was somebody older and vaguely repulsive who tried

to put his hand against your thigh in the public library, then started

to follow you out at closing time, talking about Gide and Rimbaud and "my good friend,

Horatio." You tried to flee, or so you ingenuously believed at the time, but in fact

you entrapped him at the subway platform, crying out in front of police

and the businessmen and the rough construction workers, "Help, get this rotten fairy

off my back!" and they collared him and pulled him away just as you got

on your train, and you watched the dismay and the look of betrayal fill

his eyes as your train pulled out, and you caught the sadistic look in the eyes

of the tough men who held him by the arms and slapped him around and spat

in his face, shouting curses, all on your behalf. That never happened? Am I making this up?

Didn't the fellow have an accent of some kind? A peculiar lisp, a little bit of a

drool? Can't you give me any details? Did he wear a little pinky ring like this?

Did you suspect he was wearing a little rouge and mascara to make himself

attractive? He was fat, of that you're certain, is that right? And dark, in need of a shave,

with bulging eyes like Zero Mostel? Instead of my guessing, why don't you

tell me the details that you do remember? Even a single word would help.

COVER STORY

It's a point of pride with me to out-dress
my oncologist. Superficially
there's little challenge. He's committed
to the doctrine of white coat and stethoscope.

But I can heave my shoulder-padded double-
breasted blazer by Armani over the hook
and take him tie for tie, collar for collar,
shoeshine, pant cuffs, pleats in the trousers.

In the end, he trumps me:
"Put this gown on, open to the back, please."
Still, I'm the dandy he could never hope to be,
from the very surface of my skin—outward.

THE KISS

My overturned yarmulke all there was between us. Desire pressed
    us into one another, whispered "Yes!"—No Voice, no
        Person rose to challenge its demand. There was no freedom
in the silence, the darkness. There was your mouth, full of matches, my
    rags of gasoline.

POSTCARD

I took your postcard to Jerusalem.
My tongue clove to my palate.
My right arm withered.
I could not forget you.

I visited the Wall. I had come
to cry King David's songs
in King David's language
with my own mouth.

At the *mikvah* I paid for the towel
and folded my clothes.
I placed my ring in one of my shoes,
my father's watch in the other.

My glasses clouded. I removed them.
Naked, I waited
for the crowded shower.
It was you I wanted.

BROKEN VESSEL

I have not been castrated!
Laugh—but to me, what a relief—
my cock and both my balls
still there where they belong.

Blood spread on my pants so fast.
Was I just opened up
and left to bleed to death? No—
I'm intact. But blood pours through

my cock like piss only faster,
fuller without slowing.
Nothing I can do.
All the blood I'll ever have.

AFTER THE STORM

The plain is covered
with felled giant trees,
their limbs and trunks
an impenetrable woven chaos.

The dreadful sound of bees
thickens the moist air.

WILLOW GONE

Willow Gone
How Will I
No Hair Now
Woman
Go Alone

THAT OTHER COUNTRY

WHENEVER I DREAM OF MY MOTHER

I don't mind the way her faces keep changing.
Coy, threatening, bearded then bald,
nauseating, suddenly voluptuous.

Whenever I dream her, I'm passing
between worlds, no longer retained,
not yet recollected.

          "You're right!" I agree with her.
"Neither would I let my daughter be a Girl Scout
selling cookies to the neighbors.
                  Rather in her
let creation form! Grasses! Trees! The Beasts
with Names! The Constellations!"

                  However,
I never had a daughter. Nor, for that matter,
has my mother. So I must leap in her place
from the back stairs of this tenement
into the refuse of the restaurants below
and reassemble living things from leavings,
bones, and broken shells.

              "Make your mark,"
my mother mumbles through the changes of her mouth.
". . . your mark," she whimpers, spits, whispers, sneers, grins,
then disappears.

BEFORE SUNRISE

Last night the wind-whipped willow
      clattered loose her catch of stars.

The cord to the moon is cut.
      There shall be no more tides.

Now red meat hangs from this lamb's new teeth—
      He shall not be scalded in his mother's milk!

No! Never trust the child's gaze of adoration.

TOWARD THE LAND OF MORIAH
WINTER 1990-91

I close my eyes,
see That Place—far off.

The basement shelter,
doors and windows sealed,
the gas masks.

My son asked for God.
"Offered myself," is how he put it—
and now scuds
and Desert Storm.

He knows, studying Torah
in Jerusalem, he
is saving lives, not
risking his own.

His mother screams at me,
"Get him home!" Calls me
"Murderer!"

It is not my son God wants—
not his death, not his life.

It is my offering.

Not my son's life.

Mine.

LECH LECHA
(GO! TO YOURSELF!)

Outside.
Alone.
In real dark—
beyond the net of light
cast by the house,
his back to the looming roof,
all that care,
all that obligation—
here
the choked murmur rises
from tangled grasses
wakened, commanding:

"Go! To yourself—
that other country—
still unknown."

SYDNEY UNDERSTOOD

Sydney saw at once how I was making
        too much of my move away from the 5 by 8
                lined spiral notebooks I'd been writing in
for thirty years since college. He suppressed
        a smile when I told him keeping the spine
                of the new 9 by 12 unlined sketch pad
horizontal on the top would liberate
        my writing line—"more than twice as long!"—and
                that my phrasing too would open out
like Whitman, unfold with new rhythm, flight,
        sonority like later Coltrane! He
                recognized my thrill—and the fear underneath it:
breaking out of the vertical format,
        narrow page, pale green lines. Several hundred
                volumes stuffed in trans-files took more closet
space than three air conditioners. Sydney
        understood sex, being fifty, the faint
                whiff of decay, my quickened appetites,
having one son over twenty, another
        under ten, staying in the studio
                all night, the family tolerant but
dubious in the morning, my fear of
        telling, their fear of asking what I was
                working on and on and on and on. "Don't
worry," he said, "about wasting all that paper.
        You paid for it already."

SUS V'ROCHVO
(HORSE AND RIDER)

I'm tossing crumpled paper onto the path: dollar bills, pages of Gemara, tickets
      to Jerusalem, your poems, mine. I'm just opening
          my hands, letting everything fall, reaching toward the muzzle
of the animal leaping beneath my inner thighs. Obstacle of bulrushes.
      Obstacle of language. Obstacle of memory. Obstacle of stone. Horse,
        I am giving you your way, Large Horse, my eyes wide open,
stinging of your mane.

DOCTOR HOWARD

Doctor Howard wants to see my scar.
Thirteen inches of black barbed wire
wind left of my navel down
to the new-grown thatch at my groin.

In the theater, dark before the lights came on,
he stroked my hair. I leaned into his chest,
naked, shivering in the icy sterile air.
The gondolier planted the epidural—
I glided away on that cold river.

Doctor Howard sliced me open, mopped
away the blood, tied back the skin and fat,
tied back the abdominal wall, fondling
my glands and intestines wet and orange,
hot and purple, till he found the hydra
he was looking for, then severed the colon
and took his fourteen centimeters.

Weeks later now, he slides his middle
finger gloved in latex, greased
with KY, deep inside me
to evaluate the reconstructed anal verge.

My death in one hand, my life in the other,
you untangled the sticky strands
then sewed me up before you wiped
the perspiration from your brow,
lifted your little green face mask
and kissed me deeply
on the mouth to waken me.

SARAJEVO SERENADE
JULY 1992

Serb Guns— But isn't this a panoramic map of that ski resort
      my father and mother took me and my brother to
         in the nineteen-fifties: Lake Placid? Or is it Kleine Scheidegg, the pass
from Grindelwald to Wengen, where I hiked, an adult, in the season
      of what would have been my father's seventieth birthday? He appeared
         at dawn in a dream and pleaded that I apprehend
those Alps for him, with all my senses, deeply
      while avalanches rumbled off the Jungfrau. *—Bjelašnica,*
         Olympic ski slope (Bosnian-held). Trebević Mountain. Ruins
of Olympic Hall. I want to find the warming hut, the smell of fried potatoes,
      my goggles steaming up, my mother in the corner window with the chocolate,
         the extra mittens, her sketchbooks and pastels. Little Mother, how you
sit and draw and read and knit because you dread the chairlifts,
      dread steel towers, cables, all that mechanism for the sake of flirtation
         with catastrophe twisting into the speeding descent.
Hearth-mother, holding all your husband and your sons require, tell me
      how the music rises through the keening and the shrieks
         of *grandmother struck by sniper fire at the graveside of her dead*
son's daughter, two years old? I thread the cochlea
      of this ear of twisted streets to find where the music comes from
         which sustains these starving citizens who yet sit tilted slightly
forward on their stones, in their doorways, on the edges of what once were
      sidewalks, tilted into the music though they have no hair, though they have
         no eyebrows, tilted into the music though what remains of their skin

is wrinkled, wrinkled, wrinkled. Yet what lips they have
      are smiling, what eyes they have are smiling for the music they lean into,
            which sustains them while they wait for bread though there is no bread,
while they wait days, twenty-two, one day for each letter of the *Aleph-Bais*
      with which the Master of All Worlds created this world
            and the Torah. One day for each starving citizen who was killed
on the line for bread by the mortars fired from the bobsled run.
      The music comes from the cello of Smailović—Vedran—of the now-
            disbanded Sarajevo Opera. Smailović, who has dressed himself
for twenty-two days in his formal attire, stained though it is with dust and crusts
      of blood—shirtfront, starched white collar, black tie
            knotted at the throat, patent-leather shoes, a *boutonnière*—
and set up his music, Albinoni's *Adagio*, in its folding music stand
      and opened up his folding stool with the bright-colored parasol
            which protects him from the sun of July. Smailović, whom some
condemn for seeking death from the snipers shrouded in the summer
      loveliness of hillside groves, some of which were sacrificed for parking
            lots for 1984's events. But Smailović, the perfect target with his bright-
colored parasol, his refusal of silence, has loaned his body
      and his great wide cherry wood lung of a cello to the archangel Raphael,
            and for twenty-two days even I, from North America, with my well-fed
face, come in my dreams to hear his music and be sustained.

JUST AS I AM

I AM LISTENING:
LATE FRIDAY AFTERNOON

I made a recording yesterday
while a cold rain played the windows.
Two hours I read out loud without fatigue.

I'm listening to my own voice now.
A kettle with bones and vegetables
simmers over a low flame.

A twisting skein of steam escapes from roof vents
of the thirty-story Shearson building
half a mile toward the Hudson,

my own essence rising
easily with the shadows.

I'M NOT HAPPY WITH MY EYES
for Gerald Stern

If I want to see three feet away or more, my tan pair
of glasses are perfect. If I want to read or to write,
the green ones are fine. But when I want to draw or be
distracted by these people, those trees, this odd flock of dogs
now passing, or whatever it was that made me sit down
on this cold stone bench to write a poem of gratitude to Stern,
then neither tan nor green is any good at all.
I have to pull the silver ones, bifocals, out from their snapping
tortoise case which blunders somewhere down in the bottom
of my bag under notebooks, candy bars, and all my other
eyeglass cases.

                When I smoked I used to carry pipes.
Like that drooping bent-stem briar I would pack with dark moist
Lebanese or Balkan leaf to smoke while reading something
serious in a deep chair, slowly so I wouldn't often
need a hand to turn the pages. That pipe was heavy
to hold in my jaw for too long. In my palm it felt
laden, warm, like a scrotum dense with seed, the smoke
of promises hovering over my nose, my brows.

                Of course for walking,
I needed a very different kind of pipe: straight, light,
but strong enough to hold tight in my teeth, to thrust
before me into the air, to burn bright Virginia shag
or burley, navy-cut, smoke curling around my ears,
out of my hair, behind me. I am wearing a scarf,
no hat, a woolen jacket. I am probably English.

I'll say more about pipes, but right now snatches
of talk keep reaching my ears from the remarkable
women who walk through the park with their children, friends,
their wealthy retired husbands. They speak Russian,
many of them, or a musical French. One, in a dark
wool suit, black stockings, fine silk scarf, dark glasses, has deep
wrinkles, a minor scar on one slack cheek as if she'd had
a stroke and is almost entirely recovered. She
says to the tall man she is leaning against, "He was good. Fair
but tough. He was smart. A decent, honest man." I
understand her perfectly. She is talking
about my father. She's absolutely right. She means
he was angry. She means he was always disappointed.
And he was sorry everyone thought he was angry at them,
disappointed in them—which he was—but had given up
explaining, given up trying to understand.

Those days when I smoked but saw clearly, I changed
pipes as often as now I change glasses. I was addicted
to tobacco, for which I feel no shame. I changed pipes
so often—and tobacco too—because it was wonderful
how the simple pleasure of smoking had so many subtle
variations, mysteries—for the tongue, for the throat,
for the fingers, the jaw and the nostrils.

I wanted to write to Stern because the girl I watched
dropped a piece of her cookie in the sailboat pond
just a moment ago—a treat to lure the bright gold carp,
the gallant snowy swan to her corner of sunlight. But
the gulls came down, and one dull lumpy fellow snatched
at the chunk and got it just before it crumbled
in the rotten water. I wanted to write to Stern,
praise him for bringing that girl, that cookie crumb, that gull
together in my variously farsighted, nearsighted
eyes here in Central Park, November the eighth, with

the Russian women and French tourists, the sister
and brother-in-law taking a break from the honest, smart
patient in the hospital, the dog walkers, the high
school kids, and this purposeful gentleman in his gray
flannel slacks, loose short coat, beret. He's a musician,
a philosopher, a refugee from Poland. He once
made wondrous pieces of fine cloisonné. When I
was a student in the early nineteen sixties he
invited me to his apartment where his wife served
tea in the winter afternoon, sun streaking the sky
red over the sullen Hudson River.

                                I did not know
then and I do not know today which glasses I should wear
when I look at the person who sits before me.

I said goodbye to my father at the office door on a Friday
in '76. I see the textured globe of his woven
Rooster tie in the buttoned-down archway of his tattersall
collar. He said, "I'll see you Monday." "You won't,"
I corrected him. "It's Labor Day." "Oh, right. Drive safely."

I have tucked a handful of men into bed since then.
Or kissed them goodbye, left them in the hospital
with their own sons or nurses or wives or alone.
I would have tucked my father in, adjusted his pillow,
given him a shave, seen that his IV. didn't get tangled.
But he could not use my help. He did not suffer.
His heart gave way that weekend. Sudden. No one
could attend him. No one had to go to any trouble.
Living, he suffered. But no one could attend him, bring
little packages of mints, a nice bunch of flowers—then take
a break for a walk in the park, a pipe stuck hard
in the teeth, feet kicking at crunching leaves, the broken twigs.

THE OLDER MAN

The mornings are painful to him. The foul breath. The need
          to evacuate. The sunlight. Everything accuses.
                  I leave our bed first, quietly shower and shave,
prepare coffee, flowers on the table. I pretend I'm shy.

I pretend he's my grandfather in the Brooklyn kitchen
          on a Sunday morning. The floor is white tile, a thin
                blue border. His love is all I want. He dips
his roll deep into a bowl of cream and holds it to me.

He knows I use this memory: black seeds on the surface
          of the cream, high blue flame beneath
                the percolator, water gathering
energy till the bubbles rise to wet the grains.

I know the memories he uses.

VISITATION: LOWER MANHATTAN

I walk from the P.O. at Canal and Wooster, your letters in my pocket,
        cross Canal into lower SoHo, turn east on Grand to Little Italy,
                into Chinatown where it spills up Mulberry, overflows
the Bowery. Your voice in my ears now, I cross Allen Street into
        the neighborhood of hold-out Jewish dry goods merchants,
                discount retail clothing shops, their signs bilingual, Spanish
and Yiddish. I turn down Essex to G & M Glatt Kosher where I hang out
        with the mobs of widows, the *kvetchedicke* remnant of old-time Jews
                still living in the Grand Street Co-ops, still keeping
kosher, still keeping Shabbos, still wondering how come *they* didn't get
        a son-in-law who could make it in the suburbs and have the heart
                and the cash to set them up nice someplace in Florida.
I walk with your voice in my ears, your entire mouth—throat, jaws,
        tongue, lips, teeth—while I order "a roasted chicken,
                a quart of soup, a half dozen kreplach, and I'm here already
so you may as well give me a nice piece of whitefish, and for my son
        just one stuffed cabbage. One will be enough. And a small lokshen
                kugel. Not sweet. Salt and pepper. You don't have a small?
Okay, I'll take a medium." I hear your radials whirring
        on the mountain roads. I hear your animals poking their muzzles
                in your face. I hear your printer clattering away
like mine does, while your voice, your heart, your mind, your moisture
        breathe into my ears where I stand in the bakery waiting my turn,
                but it's been my turn already and the lady that came in
behind me has caught the counterman's attention. Which is fine.
        I'm not in any hurry. I know what I want, smelling the braided
                challahs, the mandelbroit, the yeasty babka, the sticky

mohn-cake thick with its paste of prune and poppy seeds. I want your face,
        your body. I want a week with you, the seashore, the mountains,
                the riverbank, the room in the harbor, the far West.
I am walking back along Canal Street, listening to everything you say,
        buying seven different kinds of tea in Chinatown, scallions
                and watercress from the stand that sells live carp and
turtles from a big brown tank. I'm buying lychees from the shop
        across the street where half a pig, a dozen ducks, and ropes
                of barbecued intestines hang from shining flesh hooks,
dripping fat into the wooden basin. Lunchtime. The garment workers
        gather. The man hacks off a clump of this or that and chops it
                to bits on a stump then packs it over rice, some slippery
greens, in a paper pail with a wire handle. I love the way you
        permeate my daily chores, the taste of cake and gravy flavoring
                the distances between us. What if, at last, we just fly
to the frontier, abandon our lives, and never return?

THE ESCAPE

My mother has been drinking.
She says the trouble with this life is
one must always have two faces.
Make them look the same, I say.

Someone calls out her name from the street.
She collapses hiding her face in my arm.
I carry her in to the yacht.
She must not touch the earth.

A crewman in livery
neatly cuts the cable with an axe.
We are caught by the tide,
delivered and drifted again.

Come closer to me, She says. I obey.
She produces a cord from beneath her skirt
and wraps it around my waist.
At once I am turning back into blood.

BIRCHAS HaGOMEL
(HOMECOMING)

I take my old place in the synagogue, apart from the women, apart
      from the men, wrapped up in the black-banded tallis of rough
wool I brought back from B'nai B'rak, wrapped up in the parchment
      the Breslover Sopher inscribed, dripping from the gathered pool of waters
where he had to immerse five times before he would even sharpen his quill.

      I am called to my portion. I recite the required blessing for deliverance
from danger: "Blessed are You, oh Lord, King of the Universe, Who bestows good things
      upon the guilty, Who has bestowed every goodness upon me," and the congregation
cries out its response, "*Amen!* May He Who has bestowed goodness upon you continue
      to bestow every goodness upon you forever."

                           Your red mouth closes
over me when the congregation stands. The ark is opened.
      Your white breasts beam out between the velvet dresses and the silver crowns.
I pronounce your name. The straps of *tfillin* on my arm unwind in a coil
      and rise between my feet. I reclaim you, traveler,
though I left you crumpled in a tiny fuse of paper squeezed in a crack
      between caper bush and swallows' nest in that Wall of Stone
that will not cease to rise before my eyes.

IT IS MAY

Now it is May and I'm praying for snow. April I prayed in Jerusalem,
      the jealous God of my fathers commanding: Yearn with all the heart,
            the soul, every power for The Inapprehensible alone. Another yearning
rises from the spring I've sipped from, stand at the edge of, astonished
      by my thirsting. I shall never know myself if I will not know
            her whom I summoned from my own heart's core, imploring her to enter.

Now it is May. At my window I am praying for snow, teased to unfocussed
      dumb confusion, the numberless crystals of the ceaseless swirl
            undifferentiated in my gross eye. Uncompleted songs rise
in my divided throat, urgent, uncompromising. Song to God who commands,
      "Be Holy." Song to her who offers, "Know." Now it is May. I am praying
            for snow, obliteration, for numbness, stupefying cold.

DAUGHTERS OF TIAMAT

I have collected you, letter by letter. Words. Then remembered movements
     of hip and arm. Your hot pink blouse? Forget about going to the cleaners.
          I took the ticket. Oh, none of this works as your fingernail did,
the lock of your hair, that drop of your blood—DNA for the figure I had to create
     —which still didn't serve as your actual lips, nipples, fingertips—little
          parts of your body I would nibble on or, better, big ones—buttocks,
stomach, shoulders, thighs—I could wrap myself around, press myself into. Stone,
     deserts of broken stone, frozen mountain passes, seven thousand years impose
          themselves between us. What little conjury I swallowed with my mother's
milk is what I go on. This synagogue I'm waking in is carved from soft wood
     Java-style, everything curving out and upward like palm fronds or fish fins,
          everything painted bright colors—especially yellow, a goldenrod really,
enough to make your eyes burn thirty-six years, and a lacquered purplish red
     that gleams like swollen labia. The scrolls of the Torah, as in Baghdad and
          India, curl inside their filigree sheesham wood cabinets wearing finials
of silver and brass that sing out loud from the arms of the elders when they're carried
     to the Bimah: *b'tziltzelai shamma! b'tziltzelai truah!* Little girls in white
          and yellow hide and seek in the old men's beards. The teenage boys, their
endlessly deep and serious eyes longing for, averted from, everything, shiver
     brimming in expectation. Marriages! Messiahs! Everywhere, mothers in orange
          and green silk saris throw armsful of candies, blossoms and coins.

At night I sneak those letters from a corner in my secret drawer. I bring selected
     phrases to my bedside in the darkness. Deep inside the night I chew them a little
          then press them to my nostrils to capture their aroma. I rub them against
my chest, over my belly till they slip of their own to my groin. They twine
     themselves around me, draw the wetness from me. My dreams
          —lotus and porpoise, burnt barns, concentration camps—Sex and Death
—at war. No. In alliance! Tiamat unwinds

in the purple waters stored above the sapphire
heavens, all of her daughters rising in my left hand from the seed I've spilled
in vain. Alexander quails before the High Priest of Jerusalem, scampers back
to Macedonia. Klaus Barbie manages a chain of inner-city foster homes. Every child
—brown or white—has a wet nurse of its own, its own clean bed, a view
of Caribbean beaches, blue smoke rising from the evening cook fires
along the Swannanoa, the Ganges, the Danube, the Amazon, tethered horses nibbling
sweet grain. Over the rolling green hillsides, horned and unhorned flocks
sweep like the shadows of clouds. And water. Always water
—gurgling in crevices, flowing over stones, crashing out of heaven—the sperm-sprung
daughters of Tiamat—swarming, laughing, singing with foam, fire in their purple
eyes, fire in their hot pink blouses. Star-shaped, moon-shaped, tree-shaped
bits of their tickets flicker through the air like snow from the conductor's hand
punch. *"All abo-oard!"* Our breath like the steam of Monet in the Gare St. Lazare—
we will rise from the dead! We have risen already! We must crumble, dance
—we must—all over again until there is nothing but rising. That little . . . *poupée!*
—if in your drawer, if in mine—may be all that we have to hold on to
in this storm—or that singular thing we have to be rid of to bring
The Redemption! I am crazier than ever. I have never been more sane.
I know exactly what I'm doing. I am hopelessly confused. I know nothing
will come of this ever, nothing that isn't already in bloom.

JUST AS I AM
Monday, September First

Just about noon. My back is to the sun, my face into the wind,
　　　northeast. In my vista are the dunes just up the beach from Ballston,
　　　　　　the ocean and the sky. There had been a man and a woman standing
where the mild waves lay out their winnowings along the glistening stones
　　　discovered by their slosh and drag, but the man has wandered back
　　　　　　up the beach to his blanket, where he lies, hands
underneath his head, looking up into the vacant blue sky, closing his eyes now,
　　　losing himself to sensation—sounds of the surf, heat of the sun,
　　　　　　breezes playing over his torso—and the woman, tall and beautiful,
her bikini printed with large pink apparently innocent flowers, has walked away
　　　along the water's edge, sometimes in the soft sand that is dry, sometimes
　　　　　　in the water that sucks at her ankles, sometimes on the wet hard shingle
in between, which variously resists or yields to her footfall as it holds
　　　or relinquishes the burden of the waves. The stories I imagine
　　　　　　of their conversation, the occasion for their tryst, the reasons
for their separation, are stories that haven't anything to do with them
　　　at all. Yes, I would like to meet with a beautiful woman
　　　　　　out here along the edge of the Atlantic. And also I would like
to have her walk away and leave me here alone again,
　　　just as I am.

　　　　　　Now twenty to one in the early afternoon. I have to
　　　begin all over again. (But when and for whom has it ever been
otherwise?) I was discovered by my wife and our ten-year-old and his friend.
　　　They were striding up the beach to where the boys believe the nudists
　　　　　　might be found. The boys are looking for tits and ass. My wife too,
in her way, believing the exercise will sharpen the appearance of her own. I'm settled
　　　where I am, hoping any people that I see will walk right through my field
　　　　　　of vision and not linger in the range of my attention

beyond my wish to use them for my story, as I was doing before with the man
        who was back at his blanket in the sand and the woman who was walking
                away along the border of the sea that washes Africa and Haiti,
England and the edges of the drainage basin of the Amazon. But my ten-year-old
        wanted to roll me down the embankment into the water or at least delight
                in the struggle my resistance would present,
and my wife too, in a way, wanted to do the same, making her comments
        about returning to the city or packing up the dishes and the linens.
                All I want is to sit here just as I am (though my back is getting tired)
and just to keep on writing back and forth across this twelve-inch page
        this somewhat rhythmic loping, prosy kind of poetry which isn't saying
                anything but seems, some way, to imitate the sounds
of water at the beach's edge and the visual traces that the motion
        of the waves leaves on the drying sand. It isn't that I have intention
                in this enterprise, though I'm taking pleasure as the time unwinds,
except that I expect (there! as in just this instance, this play
        between those words) to find a little fragment like a pretty
                shell or a glistening stone with peculiar streaks and a rib
of harder stuff that hasn't gotten polished by erosion as the darker, softer matrix.
        And I confess the presence of another motive. No, that's too strong a word.
                I confess a hint of hope that in this sifting back and forth, this
shuttle of my pen from one side to the other, this scripting, that the unintended
        pattern will emerge or that the weave of ordinary mind will ravel out
                and leave the warp-strung loom as naked as a harp, or that the simple
objects buried underneath the sand of ordinary mind will slowly poke
        themselves into my view, laid bare as if it were the work of tide and wind.

THANK YOU

The deepest gratitude goes to my family for their patience and understanding of the moods and habits of a poet: Peggy Eliot, my wife for nearly forty years; Jonah and Ben, my wonderful, inspiring, and gifted sons; and my mother, Masha, who encouraged, even pushed me, to fulfill myself as an artist as she did for herself.

"Art withers without fellowship." I have been abundantly sustained for the last twenty-five years thanks to Martha Rhodes, who brought me into the MFA Program for Writers at Warren Wilson College. Special thanks to my teachers there: Brooks Haxton, Marie Howe, Ken Rosen, Larry Levis, and Joan Aleshire. Above all, this book would not exist without help from writers I met while in the program and at the post-MFA summer conferences organized by Friends of Writers, Inc.: my editor, Patrick Donnelly, and for critical help on this manuscript, Bob Ayres, Jayne Benjulian, Mari Coates, Lisa Croneberg, Ellen Dudley, Helen Fremont, Marie Pavlicek-Wehrli, Francine Sterle. Thanks also to my friend Neil Flax and my current New York writer's group members: Ana Diz, Cynthia Graae, Reginetta Haboucha, Zohra Lampert, and Rachel Rippy.